Bible Places Quiz Book

Erma Reynolds

BAKER BOOK HOUSE

Grand Rapids, Michigan 49506

Copyright 1981 by
Baker Book House Company

ISBN: 0-8010-7703-6

Printed in the United States of America

1. Alphabet of Scripture Places

1. A _____ Where Achan was stoned to death
2. B _____ Place where Abraham and Abimelech made a covenant
3. C _____ Where Jesus was crucified
4. D _____ Where Joseph was thrown into a pit
5. E _____ Where Israelites found 12 wells and 70 palm trees
6. F _____ Harbor where prisoner Paul stayed several days
7. G _____ Where Joshua set up 12 symbolic stones
8. H _____ Where Aaron died
9. I _____ Aquila and Priscilla came from this country to Corinth
10. J _____ A brook where Jacob wrestled with an angel
11. K _____ Where Asa burned his mother's idol
12. L _____ Place noted for its cedars
13. M _____ Place where bitter water was made sweet
14. N _____ Where Jesus raised a widow's son
15. O _____ Gold was brought from this place to King Solomon
16. P _____ Island to which John was banished
17. Q _____ Jeremiah was released from prison here
18. R _____ Place in the wilderness where an angel found Hagar
19. S _____ Where a wise woman lived
20. T _____ Abraham's birthplace
21. U _____ Where Jesus was tempted by the devil
22. V _____ Where Lot and his daughters fled when Sodom was overthrown

2. Altars

Each person in the left-hand column built an altar at one of the places listed at the right. See if you can match them.

1. Abraham
2. Balaam
3. David
4. Elijah
5. Gideon
6. Isaac
7. Jacob
8. Joshua
9. Moses
10. Noah
11. Samuel
12. Saul

A. Mount Pisgah
B. Mount Carmel
C. Rephidim
D. Aijalon
E. Bethel
F. Jerusalem
G. Ramah
H. Mount Ararat
I. Mount Ebal
J. Ophrah
K. Shechem
L. Beersheba

3. Babylon: Gate of God

Babylon, titled "Gate of God," was considered the wonder city of the ancient world. See how many of the following questions you can answer to test your knowledge of this city.

1. Who founded Babylon?
2. What was the name of the land where it was founded?
3. What king boasted, "Is not this great Babylon, that I have built for the house of the kingdom . . . ?"
4. What tree is mentioned as growing on the banks of Babylon rivers?
5. What prophet described Babylon as the "golden city"?
6. What prophet was told by God, "the broad walls of Babylon shall be utterly broken, and her high gates shall be burned with fire"?
7. What people did God say would destroy Babylon?
8. Who sent greetings from the church at Babylon?
9. Who, in a vision, was told by an angel, "Babylon the great . . . is become the habitation of devils"?
10. How long did Revelation say it took to destroy Babylon?

4. Battlefields

1. Where did King Hadadezer lose one thousand chariots in a battle?
2. Name the barley battlefield in which Eleazar stood alone and defeated enemy Philistines.
3. In what valley did Gideon battle the Midianites?
4. Where was the battlefield located in which the Ark was captured?
5. In what valley did four kings battle five kings?
6. Name the place where Revelation says the great final battle is to be fought.
7. Where did the battle take place in which Saul and his three sons were slain?
8. What king fought on the battlefield at Ramoth-gilead, disguised as an ordinary soldier?
9. On what battlefield were 22,000 soldiers reduced to 10,000, on orders from God?
10. What king was slain on the battlefield at Megiddo?

5. "Beth" Places

"Beth" is part of the spelling of a number of places mentioned in the Bible. At the left are descriptions of associations some Scripture folk had with a "Beth" place. These are listed at the right. See if you can match them.

A. Bethshemesh
B. Bethesda
C. Bethsaida
D. Bethlehem
E. Bethpeor
F. Bethphage
G. Bethany
H. Bethshan
I. Bethabara
J. Bethel

1. Moses was buried in a valley near this place
2. Where David was anointed by Samuel
3. Here Jesus healed a man who had been lame for 38 years
4. Jeroboam set up a gold calf here
5. Lazarus was raised from the dead here
6. Where John conducted baptism
7. Jesus sent disciples here to bring a donkey and its colt
8. Philip, Andrew and Peter's hometown
9. The Ark was brought here
10. The bodies of Saul and his sons were fastened to a wall here

6. Bethel

Bethel's history includes some of the people listed in the left-hand column. See if you can match each one to its tie-in with the town.

1. Elisha
2. Jeroboam
3. Abram
4. Joshua
5. Deborah
6. David
7. Jacob
8. Amos
9. Samuel
10. Josiah

A. Burned bones on an idolatrous altar in Bethel
B. Sent part of battle loot as a gift to Bethel
C. Was warned to stop prophesying in Bethel
D. Set up a gold calf idol in Bethel
E. Dreamed of a ladder here, and named the place Bethel
F. Was mocked by little children in Bethel
G. Held court and judged in Bethel
H. Took 5,000 men and set them in ambush between Bethel and Ai
I. Made camp and built an altar near Bethel
J. Was buried beneath an oak tree near Bethel

7. Bible Places

Answer each clue with the name of a place. The last letter of each place must become the first letter of the next place. For example, Adam's home: EDEN Where the Ark stayed for a while: NOB

_____ 1. Village where Jesus turned water into wine
_____ 2. Valley where Achan was stoned to death
_____ 3. Where Samuel was buried
_____ 4. Place given Caleb for an inheritance
_____ 5. Cain fled here after murdering his brother
_____ 6. Paul was let down a wall in this city
_____ 7. A wicked city destroyed by fire and brimstone
_____ 8. Abraham entertained three angels here
_____ 9. Joseph was carried as a slave to this country
_____ 10. Hiram's kingdom

8. Bible Rivers

The Scripture people listed in the left-hand column had an association with a river, listed at the right. See if you can match them.

1. Joshua
2. Balak
3. Jeremiah
4. Ezekiel
5. Adam
6. Naaman
7. Daniel
8. Jacob
9. Sisera
10. Moses

a. Arnon
b. Chebar
c. Abana & Pharpar
d. Hiddekel
e. Jordan
f. Jabbok
g. Euphrates
h. Kishon
i. Nile
j. Pishon

9. Bird, Beast and Bug Places

1. At what place did ravens feed Elijah? _____
2. At what place did quails appear miraculously? _____
3. At what place was a dove sent out to check on ground conditions? _____
4. At what place did two bears come out of the woods and kill children? _____
5. At what place was Samson attacked by a young lion? _____
6. From what place were horses sent to Solomon? _____
7. What place did Isaiah say would be possessed by the owl, raven, pelican and porcupine? _____
8. At what place did a man eat locusts? _____
9. At what place did King Rehoboam threaten to chasten his subjects with scorpions? _____
10. At what place were there plagues of lice and flies? _____

10. Birthplaces

Match each Scripture person, listed at the left, to his birthplace, at the right.

1. Abraham
2. Paul
3. Barnabas
4. Elisha
5. Joseph
6. Jesus
7. Apollos
8. Absalom
9. Manasseh
10. Aquila

a. Pontus
b. Alexandria
c. Ur
d. Egypt
e. Tarsus
f. Abel-Meholah
g. Cyprus
h. Bethlehem
i. Padanaram
j. Hebron

11. Brooks

1. What brook did David cross when he fled from Absalom?
2. How many tired men did David leave at Besor brook?
3. Who hid beside Cherith brook?
4. What fruit gave Eshcol brook its name?
5. In their wanderings, how many years did it take the Israelites to finally get across Zered brook from Kadesh?
6. Who picked five stones from a brook at the valley of Elah to use as ammunition?
7. Who had the prophets of Baal killed at Kishon brook?
8. Who stole out at night and followed a brook, to inspect the wall of Jerusalem?
9. What brook did Jesus cross with his disciples, on his way to a garden?
10. During a drought, what two men set out to check brooks, and see if grass could be found to save their stock?

12. Burial Places

1. What judge was buried in his family plot at Ramah?
2. What king was buried in a perfumed sepulchre in the city of David?
3. What military leader was buried at the edge of his property in Timnath-heres?
4. What woman was buried on the way to Ephrath, which is Bethlehem?
5. What murdered man was buried in Hebron?
6. Where were the bodies of Saul and his sons buried?
7. Where was Joseph buried?
8. What two kings were buried in Uzza's garden?
9. What woman was buried at Kadesh?
10. What nurse was buried under an oak in the valley below Bethel?
11. In what town was Lazarus resurrected from his burial place?
12. What woman was buried in a cave in the field of Machpelah?

13. Cast-Aways

The Scripture people listed in the left-hand column were cast into the places listed at the right. See if you can match them.

1. Ishmael
2. Daniel
3. Jeremiah
4. Job
5. Shadrach, Meshach, Abednego
6. John
7. Wedding guest
8. Five kings
9. Jonah
10. Joseph

a. Into a pit
b. Into outer darkness
c. Under shrubs
d. Into the sea
e. Into a lions' den
f. Into mire
g. Into a dungeon
h. Into prison
i. Into a fiery furnace
j. Into a cave

14. Castles and Palaces

In the left-hand column are descriptions of some castles and palaces of Scripture times. Match them to the place where they were located, listed at the right.

1. Zimri went into his palace and burnt it over him at this place
2. Where Jotham built castles in the forests
3. Isaiah foretold that "thorns shall come up in her palaces"
4. Paul was brought into a castle here to save him from a mob
5. At this place a man's fingers wrote on a palace wall
6. Here a palace garden courtyard had a pavement of black, red, white and yellow marble
7. There was an ivory palace here
8. This place where David captured a castle, had its name changed later
9. Cyrus' decree concerning rebuilding the temple at Jerusalem was found in a palace here
10. Where Jeremiah foretold God would kindle a fire to burn Benhadad's palaces

A. Jerusalem
B. Zion
C. Damascus
D. Achmetha
E. Samaria
F. Tirzah
G. Shushan
H. Babylon
I. Judah
J. Idumea

15. Caves

1. What cave was the hiding place of five kings?
2. Where was the cave located that Abraham purchased for a burial site?
3. At what place did Elijah live in a cave?
4. Who went to live in a cave in the mountains with his two daughters?
5. At what place did David spare Saul's life, when he was in a cave?
6. At what place did Obadiah hide 100 prophets in a cave?
7. Under what prevailing enemy did the Israelites live in caves and dens?
8. In what cave did David gather 400 guerilla fighters?
9. At what place did Jesus find a dead man's body in a burial cave, and resurrected it?

16. Cities in Trouble

Fill in each blank with the name of a Scripture city that experienced trouble.

1. Ambushed _____ was set on fire.
2. Craftsmen started a riot in _____.
3. _____ was sown with salt and destroyed.
4. An earthquake jarred _____, doing damage to its prison.
5. _____ suffered a terrible famine.
6. The waterworks of _____ were stopped.
7. God punished the citizens of _____ with a plague of boils (emerods).
8. _____ had its city tower knocked down, and its male population killed.
9. Fire and brimstone destroyed _____ and _____.
10. The walls of _____ fell.

17. City Acrostic

In this city acrostic, first guess the city name from the clue, and place it in the blank at the right. Then, reading down, circle the first letter of each city. If your answers are correct, you'll have the name of a city where Jesus taught.

1. City where Aquila and Priscilla were tentmakers _____
2. Where disciples were first called Christians _____
3. Where Elymas the sorcerer was blinded _____
4. Where Demetrius called a meeting of silversmiths _____
5. Where Paul lived "two whole years in his own hired house" _____
6. Where Jonah was sent by God _____
7. City Joshua captured by strategem _____
8. Job's land _____
9. Where Moses made waters sweet _____

18. City Signposts

Some of our United States towns and cities have a descriptive signpost at their entrance. If this custom had been practiced in Scripture times, match the cities at the left to their descriptive signpost, listed at the right.

1. Jericho
2. Tyre
3. Zion
4. Rabbah
5. Nineveh
6. Babylon
7. Nob
8. Jerusalem
9. Tadmor
10. Hebron

A. City of Truth
B. City in the Wilderness
C. City of Palm Trees
D. City of Refuge
E. City of the Priests
F. Great City
G. City of Waters
H. The Crowning City
I. The Golden City
J. City of the Lord

19. Damascus

1. Eliezer, the steward, came from Damascus. What was his master's name?
2. What conqueror placed army garrisons in Damascus, making the Syrians pay him tribute money?
3. Who was instructed by God, "go to the wilderness of Damascus" and anoint Hazael to be king over Syria?
4. Who was given permission to establish bazaars in Damascus?
5. Who considered the Abana and Pharpar rivers of Damascus better than all the waters of Israel?
6. When Elisha visited Damascus, how many camel loads of gifts were given to him?
7. What king, while visiting Damascus, saw an unusual altar and ordered a duplicate to be built?
8. What prophet predicted Damascus would become a "ruinous heap"?
9. What was the name of the street in Damascus Ananias was told to visit?
10. Who escaped over a wall at Damascus, in a basket?

20. David's Places of Refuge

Because of Saul's jealousy, David had to become a fugitive. Hidden in each sentence is a place to which he fled. Use the word bank to help you find these places.

    Adullam   Engedi   Gath   Hareth   Maon
    Naioth   Nob   Paran   Ramah   Ziph

1. Hiram, Ahab, Omri, were all kings in Bible times.
2. The Israelites were told to gather manna each day.
3. The honey in the lion's carcass was a dull amber color.
4. David left the Ark in Obed-Edom's house for three months.
5. Ziphion, Gad's son, was also called Zephon.
6. Samuel asked, "Did you ever know me to keep a ransom or bribe?"
7. Jehoshaphat sent Elishama on a trip to teach the law to the people.
8. The Israelites went to the Philistines "to sharpen every man his share, the coulter and mattock."
9. Sarah revenged Ishmael's mocking by sending him into exile.
10. If Joshua's army had not pretended to run, Ai otherwise might have been saved.

21. Egypt

1. Who was adopted by an Egyptian princess and trained in the wisdom of the Egyptians?
2. Who, because of a famine, went to live in Egypt?
3. What prophet foretold Egypt's downfall, saying it would be uninhabited for 40 years?
4. Who fled to Egypt with his wife and young child?
5. What captive became a governor "over all the land of Egypt"?
6. Who was left in Egypt as a hostage?
7. Who had to flee to Egypt because Solomon tried to kill him?
8. What king conquered Egypt during Jehoiakim's reign?
9. Who migrated to Egypt with a group of 70 persons, consisting of family and servants?
10. What prophet was told by God to take great stones and hide them in a brick kiln at the entry of an Egyptian palace?

22. Events and Places

In the left-hand column are some unusual events of Scripture times. Match each to the place where the event occurred, listed at the right.

1. 3,000 people were baptized in one day.
2. A lad fell to his death from a third floor window and was brought back to life.
3. A queen was thrown from a window and trampled to death by horses.
4. 5,000 people were fed with five loaves of bread and two fishes.
5. Paul was attacked by a poisonous snake but was unharmed.
6. Three men, cast into a fiery furnace came out unhurt.
7. A lad killed a giant 9 feet tall.
8. Because of a prophet's prayer a great Syrian army was blinded.
9. 300 soldiers lapped water like dogs.
10. At the loud blast of trumpets, the walls of a city fell.

A. Babylon
B. Samaria
C. Bethsaida
D. Harod
E. Elah Valley
F. Jericho
G. Troas
H. Jezreel
I. Melita
J. Jerusalem

23. Fields

This quiz is about fields, the open areas beyond the enclosed gardens and vineyards of Scripture folk.

1. At what place did Abraham purchase a field to be used as a burial plot?
2. To what field did Balak take Balaam?
3. At what place did Ruth glean grain in a field?
4. At what place did a cart, carrying the Ark of the Lord, come into the field of Joshua?
5. At what place were shepherds in a field watching their flocks, when they received wonderful news from an angel?
6. At what place was the field located that Jeremiah purchased from his cousin Hanameel?
7. At what kingdom did Moses promise its king that his band of travelers would not pass through field or vineyard?
8. At what place did Rabshakeh stand in the "highway of the fuller's field?"
9. What was the name of "the field of blood," that was bought with the money Judas received for betraying Jesus?
10. At what place did young prophets go into a field to gather herbs for Elisha to use to make pottage?

24. Forests and Woods

1. Who built towers in forests?
2. Whose body was cast into a great pit in a wood?
3. Who ate forbidden honey that he found in a wood?
4. What fugitive, on the advice of prophet Gad, left Moab and came to the forest of Hareth?
5. Who built "the house of the forest of Lebanon"?
6. What keeper of the king's forest was given an order to supply timber to make beams for palace gates?
7. What prophet described a forest fire set by God?
8. Who removed his mother from being a queen, because she had made an idol in a grove?
9. Who moved his tent to the oaks of Mamre, near Hebron, and built an altar there?
10. To which tribes did Joshua give the forestland where the Perizzites and Rephaim lived?

25. Found in the Mountains

The Bible mentions a variety of things that were found on mountains. Unscramble each mixed-up word to learn the identity of some of these items.

1. As when one doth hunt a PDAGRITRE in the mountains.
2. Out of whose hills thou mayest dig ASBRS.
3. As a OANECB upon the top of a mountain.
4. Were as swift as the SORE upon the mountains.
5. Thou shalt yet plant SIVNE upon the mountains of Samaria.
6. Thou sawest that the OETNS was cut out of the mountain without hands.
7. And SEHBR of the mountain are gathered.
8. Behold, the mountain was full of HERSSO and IHRSACOT of fire.
9. And the mountains shall drop sweet NIWE.
10. My EPHES wandered through all the mountains.
11. Lift ye up a NENRAB upon the high mountain.
12. There shall be a handful of RNCO in the earth upon the top of the mountains.

26. Garden of Eden

1. In what direction did God plant the Garden of Eden?
2. How was the Garden of Eden watered?
3. Name the four branches of Eden's river.
4. Among the many trees in the garden, which one had forbidden fruit?
5. Where was this tree located in the garden?
6. Why did God put Adam in the Garden of Eden?
7. What was placed at the east of the Garden of Eden?
8. Why were these items placed there?
9. What was Ezekiel's name for the Garden of Eden?
10. What was Isaiah's name for the Garden of Eden?

27. Garden Spots

1. Where did God plant a garden?
2. At what place did Ahab want to turn a vineyard into an herb garden?
3. In what city was king Manasseh buried "in the garden of his own house"?
4. Who chose the plain of Jordan to live because it was like the "garden of the Lord"?
5. At what place did king Ahasuerus entertain with a feast in his palace garden?
6. Who sent a letter to captives in Babylon, ordering them to plant gardens?
7. What prophet mentioned a garden of cucumbers?
8. Which of Jesus' disciples was accused of being in a garden?
9. In what country were gardens watered by foot?
10. In whose garden was the body of Jesus buried in a new sepulchre?

28. Gates

Each person in the left-hand column used a gate for a purpose, listed at the right. Match them.

1. Zedekiah
2. Ezra
3. Lot
4. Absalom
5. David
6. Ephron
7. Pashur
8. Boaz
9. Samson
10. Moses

A. Stood by a gate and reviewed passing troops
B. Stood at a camp gate and asked, "Who is on the Lord's side? let him come unto me."
C. He stood at a gate and conducted the business of selling a burial plot.
D. He chose a gate as a meeting place with kinfolk to redeem land.
E. He read the law before the Water Gate.
F. He put a prisoner in stocks that were in the upper Benjamin Gate.
G. He used a gate for an escape route.
H. He carried the doors and posts of a gate to the top of a hill.
I. He stood by a city gate to win over the citizens with flattery and goodwill.
J. He chose a gate as a place to sit at sundown.

29. Geographical Match

Names of some of our United States towns and cities also appear in the Bible, but not as a geographical reference. Our country's geographical names are at the left. At the right is the Scripture mention of these words. See if you can make a match.

1. Jasper, Alabama
2. Vermilion, South Dakota
3. Homer, Louisiana
4. Philadelphia, PA
5. Temple, Texas
6. Flint, Michigan
7. Bishop, California
8. Mason, Michigan
9. Bath, Maine
10. Champaign, Illinois

A. Bricklayer who worked on David's house
B. Liquid measure, about eight gallons
C. Stone in high priest's breastplate
D. Flat open country
E. Early official of Christian church
F. Structure built by Solomon
G. Church mentioned in Revelation
H. House paint color
I. Moses got water out of this type of rock
J. A measure of about eleven bushels

30. God of the Hills

The Lord, as the "God of the hills," caused the following mountains to do various actions. From the word bank, select the word, or words, to complete each quotation, and place it in the proper blank.

     depart   flowed   melted   molten   overturneth
     quake   removed   setteth   singing   smoke
     trembled

1. The hills _____ like wax at the presence of the Lord.
2. The mountains _____ at him.
3. The mountains and the hills shall break forth before you into _____.
4. Which by his strength _____ fast the mountains.
5. He _____ the mountains by the roots.
6. He toucheth the hills, and they _____.
7. For the mountains shall _____, and the hills be _____.
8. The mountains saw thee, and they _____.
9. The mountains _____ down at thy presence.
10. And the mountains shall be _____ under him.

31. God's Commands

God commanded some Scripture folk to go to certain places. Place their name in the blank by each command.

1. Go to Nineveh, that great city and cry against it. _____
2. Get thee up into the top of Pisgah, and lift thine eyes westward, and northward, and southward, and eastward. _____
3. Go down to Keilah; for I will deliver the Palestines into thine hand. _____
4. Get thee to Zarephath, which belongeth to Zidon, and dwell there. _____
5. Go up to Bethel, and dwell there: and make there an altar. _____
6. Go into the street which is called Straight. _____
7. Go to Euphrates, and take the girdle from thence, which I commanded thee to hide there. _____
8. Go into Damascus; and there it shall be told thee of all things which are appointed for thee to do. _____
9. Take thine only son and get thee into the land of Moriah. _____
10. Arise, go up to Ai. _____

32. Hidden Cities and Towns

Hidden in each of these sentences is the name of a Bible city or town. If you have trouble finding each city, look up accompanying Scripture reference.

1. Shepherds watching their flocks saw a star suspended in the sky (Acts 9:30)
2. When the Ark was returned to Jerusalem the city rejoiced (II Sam. 24:7)
3. It was a sad occasion when the disciples gathered for the Last Supper (I Kings 2:41)
4. After Joshua's ambush in Ai, no one was left to defend the city (Luke 7:11)
5. God chose Moses to be the leader of the Israelites (I Chron. 7:28)
6. Pharoah was so dominating and cruel, God punished him with plagues (Gen. 19:24)
7. A ram, a hare, a swine, were all considered "unclean" animals (Josh. 18:25)
8. God put Adam as custodian of the garden of Eden (I Kings 20:34)
9. The Israelites were miraculously delivered from Egyptian pursuers (Acts 18:2)
10. After seeing the baby Jesus, Anna then said, the Messiah had finally come (Acts 17:16)

33. Hidden Mountains

A mountain, mentioned in Scripture, is hidden in each of the following sentences. If you have trouble locating them, look up the Scripture references.

1. The mule Balaam was riding crushed his foot against a wall (Josh. 8:30)
2. Joshua's spies in Ai regarded it as insignificant (Exod. 24:16–18)
3. The widow in Jesus' parable put her money into the treasury (Song of Sol. 4:8)
4. David planned to use iron for nails in the Temple (Gen. 36:8)
5. The one book Hilkiah found was delivered to the king (Deut. 34:1)
6. Moses was chosen to be the Lord's mouthpiece (I Sam. 13:2)
7. Two Amorite kings were driven out by hornets (Num. 20:25)
8. Jehoiada, the priest, put a bored hole in a chest (Judg. 4:6)
9. "Over water, sand, crag, I lead my people," said Moses (Gen. 31:23)
10. Naomi took the name Mara rather than use her original name (Gen. 8:4)

34. High Places

Some Scripture folk who had an association with a high place are listed at the left. The mountains, or hills, are at the right. See if you can match them.

1. Noah's ark landed here
2. Where Solomon built a temple
3. Joshua was buried here
4. The bodies of Saul and his three sons were found here
5. David climbed this mount barefooted
6. Place of Aaron's death
7. Elisha met a Shunammite woman here
8. Balak and Balaam came to this high place
9. Where Moses spoke with God
10. Where Elijah experienced an earthquake

A. Mount Horeb
B. Mount Carmel
C. Mount Ararat
D. Mount Sinai
E. Mount Moriah
F. Mount Gilboah
G. Mount Ephraim
H. Mount Hor
I. Mount of Olives
J. Mount Pisgah

35. Hills in Prophecy

Some Scripture prophets made reference to hills in their prophecies. From the word bank, select a word, or words, that will fit into the blank and complete each prophecy.

     bow   break   crashing   fall   flow   lifted up
     low   melt   moved lightly   removed

1. Every mountain and hill shall be made _____.
2. I beheld the mountains and lo they trembled and all the hills ____ ____.
3. For the mountains shall depart and the hills be _____.
4. And it shall come to pass in that day, saith the Lord, that there shall be the noise of a cry from the fish gate.... and a great _____ from the hills.
5. Behold, the days come, saith the Lord.... and all the hills shall _____.
6. The hills shall _____ forth before you into singing.
7. The everlasting mountains were scattered, the perpetual hills did _____.
8. They shall say to the mountains, cover us; and to the hills, _____ on us.
9. And it shall come to pass in that day, that... the hills shall _____ with milk.
10. For the day of the Lord of hosts shall be upon... all the hills that are ____ ____.

36. Hometowns

Match each person in the left-hand column to their hometown, listed at the right.

1. Dorcas
2. Amos
3. Rahab
4. Jeremiah
5. Mary & Martha
6. Cornelius
7. Joseph & Mary
8. Huldah
9. Samuel
10. Andrew & Peter

A. Caesarea
B. Jerusalem
C. Anathoth
D. Ramah
E. Nazareth
F. Bethsaida
G. Tekoa
H. Jericho
I. Bethany
J. Joppa

37. Who Said It?

Each person in the left-hand column made a statement, mentioning a place. Match each one to his remark, listed at the right.

1. Nebuchadnezzar
2. Jeremiah
3. Hiram
4. Caleb
5. Ezra
6. David
7. Jacob
8. Paul
9. Nathanael
10. Naaman

A. Oh, that one would give me a drink... of the well of Bethlehem.

B. Then after three years I went up to Jerusalem to see Peter, and abode with him fifteen days.

C. He that smiteth Kirjath-sepher, and taketh it, to him will I give Achsah my daughter to wife.

D. Can there any good thing come out of Nazareth?

E. Bury me not, I pray thee, in Egypt.

F. Are not Abana and Pharpar, rivers of Damascus, better than all the waters of Israel?

G. Is there no balm in Gilead; is there no physician there?

H. And we will cut wood out of Lebanon, as much thou shalt need.

I. I gathered them together to the river that runneth to Ahava; and there abode we in tents three days.

J. Is not this great Babylon that I have built?

38. Wilderness Places

From the word bank select a wilderness place to fill in the blank in each statement.

> Beersheba   Damascus   Gibeon   Jeruel
> Judea   Kadesh   Maon   Paran   Shur
> Sinai

1. Abishai and Joab, pursuing Abner, caught up with him at the wilderness of _____.
2. King Jehoshaphat defeated his foes, with God's help, in the wilderness of _____.
3. The first stopping place of the Israelites, after crossing the Red Sea, was at the wilderness of _____.
4. Hagar and her son wandered in the wilderness of _____.
5. Ishmael grew up in the wilderness of _____.
6. Nadab and Abihu offered strange fire in the wilderness of _____.
7. Saul pursued David in the wilderness of _____.
8. John the Baptist preached in the wilderness of _____.
9. God told Elijah to return to the wilderness of _____, and upon arriving there to anoint Hazael king of Syria.
10. In a Psalm, David said, "the Lord shaketh the wilderness of _____."

39. How Long?

1. How long did Ezekiel sit among the Jewish exiles at the river Chebar?
2. How long was the Ark of the Lord in Kirjath-jearim?
3. How long was Paul blind in Damascus?
4. How long did the Israelites live in Egypt before starting their exodus?
5. How long did Moses' spies search Canaan?
6. How long did Joshua and his army march around Jericho?
7. How long did it take Nehemiah to complete Jerusalem's wall?
8. How long was Absalom in Gesher?
9. How long, according to Revelation, did it take to destroy Babylon?

40. In the Valleys

Hidden in each sentence is the name of a valley mentioned in the Bible. Use the word bank to help you find these hidden names.

Achor	Baca	Elah	Eshcol	Hebron
Keziz	Lebanon	Salt	Shaveh	Sorek

1. Cymbals, psalteries and harps were used at the dedication of Jerusalem's wall.
2. David was a heartsore king when he heard of Absalom's death.
3. The bronze-colored horse in Zechariah's vision walked to and fro.
4. Nehemiah put a mercantile ban on selling in Jerusalem on the Sabbath.
5. Satan gave Job a case of boils.
6. Carmel, a high place, was where Elijah defeated Baal prophets.
7. Haman's wife Zeresh, colluded with her husband against Mordecai.
8. Jehoshaphat was told to make Ziz a battleground against the enemy.
9. David ordered a chorus of singers to supply music in the Temple.
10. Archaeologists have hunted for the site of the Garden of Eden.

41. Israelites' Wilderness Wandering

One of the outstanding events related in Scripture is the 40-year wandering of the Israelites. At the left are 10 places included in their itinerary, and at the right, events that happened to the wanderers at these locations. See if you can match them.

1. Marah
2. Elim
3. Wilderness of Sin
4. Kibroth-Hattaavah
5. Hazeroth
6. Paran
7. Meribah
8. Rephidim
9. Mount Sinai
10. Mount Nebo

A. Israelites given Ten Commandments here.
B. God smote the Israelites with a terrible plague here
C. Bitter waters sweetened here
D. Israelites fought Amalekites here
E. Quail and manna miraculously supplied here
F. Moses died here
G. 12 wells and 70 palm trees found at this watering place
H. Spies sent from here to search Canaan
I. Moses struck a rock here and got needed water
J. Miriam became leprous here

42. Jericho

Match each person in the left-hand column to an incident that happened to him at Jericho.

1. Elisha
2. Joshua
3. Bartimaeus
4. Zedekiah
5. Hiel
6. Rahab
7. Elijah
8. Eglon
9. Zacchaeus
10. David

A. He told his men to stay at Jericho until their cut-off beards grew out.

B. He made his departure from Jericho by whirlwind into heaven.

C. He purified Jericho's waters.

D. He entertained Jesus in Jericho.

E. He met the "captain of the host of the Lord" at Jericho.

F. He was taken prisoner by Chaldeans in the plains of Jericho.

G. He had his sight restored at Jericho by Jesus.

H. This person's life was spared when Jericho was destroyed.

I. He rebuilt Jericho.

J. He took possession of Jericho and was murdered there later.

43. Jerusalem
The Golden

1. What tribe was alloted Jerusalem?
2. What was Jerusalem's early name?
3. Who defeated the Jebusites and made Jerusalem his capital?
4. During the period of what king was there a building boom in Jerusalem, including a magnificent temple and palace?
5. What Egyptian king "came up against Jerusalem" and robbed the temple and palace of their treasures?
6. Who built towers in Jerusalem?
7. Who made an aqueduct for Jerusalem?
8. What king destroyed Jerusalem, carrying into exile its leading citizens?
9. What book of the Bible describes Jerusalem's walls and the rebuilding of them?
10. What weeping prophet foretold the desolation of Jerusalem, and because of his prophetic words was cast into prison?

44. Jerusalem's Gates

City gates in Scripture times were important. Jerusalem, in particular, had numerous gates. The names of some of these are hidden in the following sentences. To help you, their names are listed in the word bank.

```
corner   dung   east    first   fish
horse    king   old     sheep   water
```

1. Fir strips were used in the construction of Solomon's temple.
2. Jabez called on God, asking that he enlarge his coast.
3. The rain came as the Israelites were ready to harvest their wheat.
4. After Jesus healed a man, people asked, "Was he epileptic?"
5. The Israelites, disobeying the law, ate rabbit meat.
6. Jeremiah, the prophet, was cast into a dungeon.
7. The Pharisees considered the Sabbath eating of corn erring behavior.
8. Neither Japheth or Seth were firstborn sons.
9. If Ishmael's mother had not seen a miraculous well, her son would have died of thirst.
10. Neither shall the shepherds make their fold there.

45. Jesus' Miracles Geographically

In the left-hand column are some of Jesus' miracles. At the right, places where they occurred. See if you can match them.

1. Turned water into wine
2. Raised Lazarus from the dead
3. Healed Peter's mother-in-law of fever
4. Raised the widow's son from the dead
5. Miraculous draught of fishes
6. Cured a demon-possessed man
7. Healed a deaf and dumb man
8. Gave sight to a blind man
9. Cleansed 10 lepers
10. Healed a man who had been ill for 38 years

A. Bethany
B. Bethsaida
C. Cana
D. Capernaum
E. Decapolis
F. Gadarenes
G. Jerusalem
H. Lake Gennesaret
I. Nain
J. Samaria

46. "K" Places

The letter "K" is said to be the least used letter of the alphabet, but it was often used in the spelling of Bible places. Match each "K" place at the left, to its description, listed at the right.

1. Kadesh
2. Kibroth-hattaavah
3. Kidron
4. Karkor
5. Kirjath-jearim
6. Kedesh
7. Kabzeel
8. Kishon
9. Keilah
10. Kirjath-sepher

A. Deborah and Barak gathered an army here
B. Elijah killed prophets of Baal here
C. Gideon defeated Midian hosts here
D. David rescued this place from the Philistines
E. Benaiah's hometown
F. Othniel conquered this place and received a bride for a reward
G. Israelites were miraculously fed with quails here
H. Asa burnt his mother's idol by this brook
I. Ark of the Lord was kept here for 20 years
J. Miriam died and was buried here

47. Land 'Em in Their Land

Place the persons listed in the left-hand column in the land that had a meaning for them, listed at right.

A. Nod
B. Uz
C. Moriah
D. Zuph
E. Gennesaret
F. Galilee
G. Goshen
H. Canaan
I. Moab
J. Armenia

1. God told Abraham to offer his son as a sacrifice here
2. Jesus and the disciples came here after He walked on water
3. Saul looked for lost mules in this land
4. Hiram was given a gift of 20 cities in this land
5. Cain fled to this land after murdering his brother
6. Sennacherib's murderous sons escaped to this land
7. Job's native land
8. Moses died here
9. Caleb was sent to spy in this land
10. Jacob and his family left Canaan to settle here

48. Land of Canaan

The land of Canaan has been designated in the Bible by more than one name. Unscramble the following words to learn these varied names.

1. AMMLINEU   (Isa. 8:8)
2. BERHSWE   (Gen. 40:15)
3. ROLSD   (Hos. 9:3)
4. MOSPERI   (Heb. 11:9)
5. IERSAL   (I Sam. 13:19)
6. PESNTALAI   (Exod. 15:14)
7. OHYL   (Zech. 2:12)
8. RISOOULG   (Dan. 11:16)
9. WEJS   (Acts 10:39)
10. EALUBH   (Isa. 62:4)

49. Little Town of Bethlehem

Bethlehem is probably best known as Jesus' birthplace, but the following questions relate to some other Biblical associations with this town.

1. Who went to Bethlehem for tax purposes?
2. What two women arrived at Bethlehem at the start of a barley season?
3. Who came to Bethlehem, on orders from God, in search of a future king?
4. What prophet foretold that Jesus would be born at Bethlehem?
5. What king built Bethlehem as a fortified city?
6. What murdered man's body was brought to Bethlehem to be buried in his father's sepulchre?
7. What horrible crime did Herod commit at Bethlehem?
8. Who was a wealthy farmer in Bethlehem?
9. What woman was buried near Bethlehem, and her grave marker still stands?
10. Who longed for a drink of water from Bethlehem's wells?

50. New Jerusalem

Revelation contains a symbolical description of New Jerusalem. Show your knowledge of this city by answering the following questions.

1. Where, in John's vision, did the New Jerusalem come from?
2. What was the city made of?
3. What surrounded the city?
4. What was its wall made of?
5. How many foundations did the wall have?
6. What were the foundations of the wall "garnished" with?
7. Whose names were inscribed in the wall's foundations?
8. How many gates did the city have?
9. What were the gates made of?
10. What was the material of the city's main street?
11. What building was missing?
12. What did the city have no need of?

51. Nineveh

1. Who founded Nineveh?
2. What king made Nineveh his royal residence and chief city of the empire?
3. Who was told by God, "Arise, go to Nineveh, that great city"?
4. How many days was it predicted it would take to overthrow Nineveh?
5. When the king of Nineveh heard this prediction, what did he do?
6. What was God's count of the population of Nineveh?
7. The book of what prophet describes a vision from God concerning the impending doom of Nineveh?
8. How was it predicted the city would be ruined?
9. What other prophet foretold and he "will make Nineveh a desolation, and dry like a wilderness"?
10. Who, long years later, made mention of Nineveh's repentance?

52. Pa and Ma Places

The spelling of some Biblical places start with "PA" or "MA". See how many blanks you can fill in after being cued with the clues.

1. John was an exile at this place — Pa - - - -
2. Dwelling place of Nabal — Ma - -
3. Spies went into Canaan from here — Pa - - -
4. Abraham entertained three angels here — Ma - - -
5. Paul and Barnabas met a sorcerer at this place — Pa - - - -
6. Moses made bitter waters sweet here — Ma - - -
7. Jacob was sent here to find a bride — Pa - - - - - - - -
8. Abraham purchased a burial place here — Ma - - - - - - -
9. John Mark separated from Paul and Barnabas here — Pa - - - - - - -
10. In a dream, Paul was asked to come and help this place — Ma - - - - - - -

53. Pillars

Pillars of Scripture times were in varied forms, and erected for various reasons. See if you can answer these questions concerning some of these monuments.

1. Who set up a memorial stone between Mizpah and Shen, and named it Ebenezer?
2. Who built an altar with 12 pillars, under a hill?
3. What woman's grave, near Bethlehem, was marked by a pillar that still stands today?
4. Who set up a pillar in King's Valley, giving it his own name because he had no son to erect such a stone in his memory?
5. What were the names of the two pillars that stood at the porch entrance of Solomon's Temple?
6. Who was made king of Israel by "the pillar that was in Shechem"?
7. Who took a stone that he had used for a pillow and set it up as a memorial pillar?
8. Who held a sacrifice of animals at the Stone of Zoheleth?
9. What prophet foretold there shall "be an altar to the Lord in the midst of the land of Egypt, and a pillar at the border thereof to the Lord"?
10. What father-in-law and son-in-law set up a stone pillar as witness to a covenant between them, and called it 'Mizpah' "?

54. Place Names in Threes

The answer to each clue is a place whose spelling is made up of three letters.

1. Land to which Cain fled after murdering Abel. _____
2. Wilderness searched by spies sent out by Moses. _____
3. Mount where Aaron died. _____
4. City where Doeg killed priests. _____
5. Jacob built an altar here. _____
6. Where Jeroboam set up a golden calf. _____
7. The king of Assyria deported captives to this place. _____
8. Plain where Nehemiah was asked to meet with Sanballet and Geshem. _____
9. Wilderness where the Israelites asked for bread. _____
10. Land to which Jephthah fled, and collected a band of rebels. _____

55. Places of Disaster

Terrible disasters occurred in some Scripture places, and these questions concern them. How many can you answer correctly?

1. At what place were 18 men crushed when a tower fell?
2. At what place did Samson pull down a temple, crushing thousands of people?
3. At what royal city were 12,000 of its citizens slain by Joshua's army?
4. At what place did Abimelech kill his 70 brothers on one stone?
5. At what place did Elijah execute 450 Baal prophets?
6. At what place were 27,000 men killed when a wall fell?
7. At what place were all children from age two and under killed on orders from Herod?
8. At what place was an entire army drowned?
9. At what place did 14,700 Israelites die of plague because they murmured against their leaders?
10. At what place did deceitful Ishmael and his men murder 70 men and throw their bodies into a pit?

56. Places of Kings

Fill in each blank with the name of the king who matches the accompanying clue.

1. D_____ d   hid in a cave at Adullam
2. J_____ m   set up a gold calf at Bethel
3. U_____ h   set up vineyards at Carmel
4. A_____ z   while visiting Damascus saw an unusual altar that he had copied
5. P_____ h   owned and controlled Egypt
6. I_____ h   was made king of Gilead by Abner
7. S_____ n   built store cities in Hamath
8. N_____ r   besieged Jerusalem
9. A_____ a   burned his mother's idol at Kidron Brook
10. A_____ h   fled to Lachish and was killed there
11. J_____ h   was killed in battle at Meggido
12. S_____ b   while living at Nineveh was murdered by his two sons

57. Plains

1. Who was asked to meet Sanballat and Geshem in the plains of Ono?
2. What king had a huge gold image set up in the plain of Dura?
3. Who set up residence in the plain of Mamre?
4. Who was told he would meet three men carrying kids, bread and wine, at the plain of Tabor?
5. Whose army of 40,000 men gathered in the plains of Jericho?
6. Who climbed from the plains of Moab to the top of Pisgah peak?
7. Who told Zadok "I will tarry in the plain of The Wilderness"?
8. Who chose the plain of Jordan as a place to live because it "was well watered"?
9. What Kenite pitched his tent in the plain of Zaanaim?
10. In what plain, in clay ground, did Solomon have brass pieces cast for his temple?

58. Pools

Match each pool at the left to its description, at the right.

1. Siloam
2. King's pool
3. Hebron
4. Samaria
5. Upper pool
6. Heshbon
7. Gibeon
8. Bethesda
9. Lower pool
10. Egypt's pool

A. Slain Ahab's chariot and armor were washed at this pool.
B. An angel "troubled the water" of this pool.
C. Aaron turned this pool into blood.
D. Isaiah mentioned people gathering together by this pool's waters.
E. Abner and Joab's soldiers had a sword contest at this pool.
F. A blind man recovered his sight at this pool.
G. Solomon compared this pool to beautiful eyes.
H. A truce delegation met Hezekiah's representatives by this pool.
I. Nehemiah visited this pool at night.
J. The bodies of Rechab and Baanah were hung at this pool.

59. Prophet Places

Put the name of a prophet in each of the blank spaces.

1. _____ Purified Jericho's waters.
2. _____ Sat among captives by the river Chebar.
3. _____ Was ordered to go to Nineveh.
4. _____ Hid a linen girdle in a rock by the river Euphrates.
5. _____ Opened his window toward Jerusalem when he prayed.
6. _____ Was fed by ravens at Cherith brook.
7. _____ Was a herdman of Tekoa.
8. _____ Foretold: "Shall there be a highway out of Egypt to Assyria."
9. _____ Quoted God as saying, "I will make Samaria as an heap of the field."
10. _____ Had a vision from God concerning Edom.

60. River Jordan

This quiz concerns events that occurred at the river Jordan.

1. What general cured his leprosy by washing seven times in the Jordan?
2. Who was baptized in the river Jordan?
3. Who caused an iron ax head to float in the river Jordan?
4. Who crossed the Jordan with 300 men?
5. Who built a monument of 12 stones in the middle of the Jordan?
6. Who hit the waters of the Jordan with his cloak, causing it to divide?
7. How many times was the river Jordan miraculously divided?
8. Who crossed the river Jordan in a ferry boat?
9. Whose army seized the fords of the Jordan, and at that spot killed about 10,000 Moabites?
10. Who was forbidden by God to cross the Jordan?

61. Rivers of the Bible

Using the word bank to help you, see if you can find a river hiding in each of the following sentences.

    Abana   Ahava   Arnon   Chebar   Gihon
    Kanah   Kishon   Pharpar   Pishon   Ulai

1. Kish, on learning his donkeys were lost, sent Saul to look for them.
2. Nadab and Abihu laid strange fire before God.
3. "With banners and flag, I honor God," said David in a Psalm.
4. A man in one of Jesus' parables decided the barn on his property was too small.
5. When Saul was keyed-up, harp arrangements, played by David, soothed him.
6. An affliction which made him ache, barred the man in Jesus' parable from walking.
7. A copyist mistook Anah for a daughter instead of a son of Zibeon.
8. Admah, a valley town, was destroyed with Sodom and Gomorrah.
9. "Your material and help is honestly needed," Solomon told Hiram.
10. A ban at the Garden of Eden forbade the eating of certain fruit.

62. Sacred Places

1. Where was Moses when God told him to take off his shoes because he was standing on holy ground?
2. Where did Jacob erect a stone pillar to mark the place where God had spoken to him?
3. Where was Solomon's temple built?
4. To commemorate his encounter with the "angel of the Lord" where did Gideon build an altar?
5. What mount was described as the "mountain of blessing"?
6. After the Israelites crossed the Jordan, where was the Tabernacle located?
7. Where was the temple located that king Uzziah profaned by burning incense on its altar?
8. Where was Joshua when the "captain of the host of the Lord" told him to remove his shoes because "the place whereon thou standest is holy"?
9. Where did David pitch a tent and prepare a place for the Ark of the Lord?
10. Where did Elijah conduct a contest with Baal priests, using the Lord's altar for his experiment?

63. Samaria

1. Who bought the hill of Samaria and built a city on it?
2. What king built a temple and altar for Baal at Samaria?
3. What two kings sat on a throne in the entrance of Samaria's gate?
4. What king fell from an upper window of his home at Samaria?
5. What prophet led invading Syrians, miraculously smitten with blindness, into Samaria?
6. What king besieged Samaria, causing a famine there?
7. How many lepers sat at Samaria's gate?
8. What prophet quoted God as saying, "therefore I will make Samaria as an heap of the field"?
9. What three apostles visited Samaria?
10. Who "used sorcery and bewitched the people of Samaria"?

64. Scrambled Countries

Unscramble the countries in the left. Then, match each to its clue, listed at the right.

1. PTYGE
2. AYSIR
3. SOTAMIOPAEM
4. HIOPR
5. AYTLI
6. MREAAIN
7. AAIRBA
8. HTEIOAPI
9. ANIMDECAO
10. BOMA

A. This country asked Paul to "come ... and help us"
B. Kings and governors of this country brought gold to Solomon
C. Gold was brought from here
D. Sennacherib's murderers fled to this country
E. David took his parents to this country for safety
F. Ebedmelech, who rescued Jeremiah from prison, came from here
G. Naaman was "captain of the host" in this country
H. Ammonites hired chariots and horsemen from this country
I. Aquila and Priscilla came from here
J. Jacob sent his sons to this country to buy corn

65. Scrambled Islands

Numerous islands are mentioned in the New Testament. Each of the following sentences contains the name of one of these islands, but its spelling is scrambled. See how many you can decipher.

1. I . . . was in the isle that is called TPSAOM.
2. From thence they sailed to UPCSYR.
3. Running under a certain island called CUDLAA.
4. We came with a straight course . . . unto OERSDH.
5. We sailed thence, and came the next day over against ISCHO.
6. When we had sailed slowly many days . . . we sailed under TERCE.
7. When they were escaped, then they knew the island was called LAEMIT.
8. And the next day we arrived at OMSAS.
9. We came with a straight course unto OCS.
10. We came with a straight course to MHRACIOTAAS.

66. Seas

"The gathering together of the waters called he seas" (Gen. 1:10). This quiz is about some of these seas mentioned in the Bible.

1. On what day did God create the seas?
2. The Valley of Siddim was another name for what sea?
3. Who sang about an army being drowned in the Red Sea?
4. What variety of trees were brought from Lebanon to the Sea of Joppa?
5. What prophet mentioned the Sea of Jazer?
6. On what sea did Jesus walk on the water?
7. At what sea did Jesus appear again to his disciples?
8. What was the name of the sea in which Paul was "driven up and down" for 14 days?
9. Who had a vision of a "sea of glass like unto crystal"?
10. These names all refer to a chief sea of Scripture times—Great Sea (Num. 34:6) Uttermost Sea (Deut. 11:24) Sea of the Philistines (Exod. 23:31) Hinder Sea (Zech. 14:8) What is this sea's present-day name?

67. Streets

1. What two kings made a covenant concerning the construction of streets in Damascus?
2. The bodies of what two men were stolen from the street of Bethshan?
3. Who was given a daily ration of bread from Bakers street?
4. Who had a vision of a street made of pure gold?
5. Who was instructed by God to go into a street called Straight?
6. What king brought in priests and Levites, and gathered them together "into the east street"?
7. What prophet said city streets would be full of boys and girls at play?
8. What man was told by angels that they would prefer to spend the night in the street?
9. Who gave orders not to publish news of the death of a father and son in the streets of Askelon?
10. What escaped prisoner was led through a street by an angel?
11. Who read a book of the law to people who had gathered in the street before a gate?
12. Who, when he prepared a seat in the street, young men hid, and the aged stood up?

68. The Name was Changed

In Scripture times some places had their names changed. Listed at the left are the original names. See if you can match each to its changed name, listed at the right.

1. Luz
2. Laish
3. Kirjath-arba
4. Bela
5. Ephrath
6. Kirjath-sepher
7. Zion
8. Zephath
9. Jebus
10. Hazazon-tamar

A. Debir
B. Hebron
C. Jerusalem
D. City of David
E. Bethel
F. Hormah
G. Engedi
H. Dan
I. Zoar
J. Bethlehem

69. Towers

Unscramble the mixed-up letters in each sentence so they will spell the name of a Scripture tower.

1. Israel journeyed and spread his tent beyond the tower of ADRE.
2. From the tower of NESYE, even unto the border of Ethiopia.
3. And he beat down the tower of EEUNPL and slew the men of the city.
4. The city shall be built from the tower of HLENEANA unto the gate of the corner.
5. Thy neck is like the tower of VADDI.
6. Or those eighteen upon whom the tower in AMILOS fell.
7. The watchman was standing on the tower in EZJELRE.
8. When all the men of the tower of EHCSMEH heard thereof they entered the stronghold.
9. Above the fish gate . . . and the tower of AHEM.
10. Thy nose is as the tower of LNOEABN.

70. Unusual Sights

Match each unusual sight, listed at the left, to the place where it happened, listed at the right.

1. Sun standing still
2. Brilliant light from heaven blinding a man
3. Floating iron ax head
4. Burning bush
5. Rod turning into a serpent
6. Bees and honey in a lion's carcass
7. Mountain filled with horses and chariots of fire
8. Water gushing from a rock
9. Handwriting on a wall
10. Great sheet, let down from heaven, filled with all kinds of animals

A. Dothan
B. Horeb
C. Timnath
D. near Damascus
E. Joppa
F. Babylon
G. Gibeon
H. Jordan
I. Egypt
J. Horeb

71. Watering Places

Water was scarce and greatly valued in Scripture times, and this quiz is about some of the watering places.

1. At what well did Gideon have his men lap water like dogs?
2. At what brook did God tell Elijah to hide and drink its water?
3. At what place did the Israelites find 12 wells?
4. At what place did Lot choose to live because it "was well watered"?
5. At what place did Hezekiah make a pool, a conduit, and brought water to the city?
6. At what place did Elisha use salt to heal the waters of a spring?
7. At what place were Jonathan and Ahimaaz hidden in a well?
8. At what pool did an angel "trouble the water"?
9. At what place did Isaac's servants dig, and find a well of "springing water"?
10. At what place was a servant given a drink at "a fountain of water" by a beautiful girl?

72. What was Where?

In the left-hand column are some unusual items of Scripture times. Match each to the place where it was located, listed at the right.

1. Brass serpent on a pole
2. Ladder reaching to heaven
3. Altar of 12 pillars
4. Tree of knowledge
5. Silver shrine for a goddess
6. A 12 stone memorial
7. Iron bedstead
8. Golden statue, 90 feet high and 9 feet wide
9. Chest with a hole in its lid
10. Seven altars in one place

A. Pisgah
B. Jordan
C. Dura
D. Bethel
E. Rabbah
F. Edom
G. Jerusalem
H. Eden
I. Mt. Sinai
J. Ephesus

73. Where?

Where were the following places? Match each description to its place.

1. A street called Straight
2. House upon a wall
3. Garden of God
4. The ivory house
5. Tower with its top in heaven
6. His own hired house
7. Burning fiery furnace
8. The field of blood
9. House by the seaside
10. Receipt of custom

A. Babylon
B. Jerusalem
C. Rome
D. Jericho
E. Capernaum
F. Joppa
G. Damascus
H. Eden
I. land of Shinar
J. Samaria

74. Why?

1. Why did Hebron become Caleb's inheritance?
2. Why did the work of re-building the Temple in Jerusalem stop for a while?
3. Why did the citizens of Lydda turn to God?
4. Why did John the Baptist choose Aenon as a baptismal site?
5. Why were the men of Ephraim offended by Jephthah?
6. Why were Agrippa and Bernice in Caesarea at the time of Paul's trial?
7. Why was Paul brought to Caesarea by the disciples?
8. Why did Jesus choose Capernaum as a place to live?
9. Why did Joseph's five brothers want permission to live in Goshen?
10. Why did Solomon choose Moriah as the site for his temple?
11. Why did Jesus' parents settle in Nazareth on their return from Egypt?
12. Why were Paul and Silas imprisoned at Philippi?

ANSWERS

1. Alphabet of Scripture Places

1. Achor (Josh. 7:24)
2. Beersheba (Gen. 21:27-32)
3. Calvary (Luke 23:33)
4. Dothan (Gen. 37:17-24)
5. Elim (Exod. 15:27)
6. Fair Havens (Acts 27:8)
7. Gilgal (Josh. 4:20)
8. Hor (Deut. 32:50)
9. Italy (Acts 18:2)
10. Jabbok (Gen. 32:22-24)
11. Kidron (I Kings 15:13)
12. Lebanon (I Kings 5:6)
13. Marah (Exod. 15:22-25)
14. Nain (Luke 7:11-15)
15. Ophir (I Kings 9:28)
16. Patmos (Rev. 1:9)
17. Ramah (Jer. 40:1)
18. Shur (Gen. 16:7)
19. Tekoa (II Sam. 14:2)
20. Ur (Gen. 11:28)
21. Wilderness (Matt. 4:1)
22. Zoar (Gen. 19:20-23)

2. Altars

1. K (Gen. 12:6, 7)
2. A (Num. 23:14)
3. F (II Sam. 24:16, 25)
4. B (I Kings 18:19, 31, 32)
5. J (Judg. 6:11, 24)
6. L (Gen. 26:23, 25)
7. E (Gen. 35:6, 7)
8. I (Josh. 8:30)
9. C (Exod. 17:8, 15)
10. H (Gen. 8:4, 20)
11. G (I Sam. 7:17)
12. D (I Sam. 14:31, 35)

3. Babylon: Gate of God

1. Nimrod (Gen. 10:8, 10)
2. Shinar (Gen. 10:10)
3. Nebuchadnezzar (Dan. 4:30, 31)
4. willows (Ps. 137:1, 2)
5. Isaiah (Isa. 14:4)
6. Jeremiah (Jer. 51:58)
7. Medes (Isa. 13:17-22)
8. Peter (I Peter 5:13)
9. John (Rev. 18:1, 2)
10. one hour (Rev. 18:19)

4. Battlefields

1. river Euphrates (II Sam. 8:3, 4)
2. Pasdammin (I Chron. 11:12-14)
3. Jezreel (Judg. 6:33, 34)
4. Ebenezer (I Sam. 4:1-11)
5. valley of Siddim (Gen. 14:1-9)
6. Armageddon (Rev. 16:16)
7. Mount Gilboa (I Sam. 31:1-6)
8. Ahab (I King 22:29, 30)
9. Harod (Judg. 7:1-3)
10. Josiah (II Kings 23:28, 29)

5. "Beth" Places

1. E (Deut. 34:5, 6)
2. D (I Sam. 16:4-13)
3. B (John 5:2, 5-9)
4. J (I Kings 12:25-29)
5. G (John 11:1-44)
6. I (John 1:28)
7. F (Matt. 21:1, 2)
8. C (John 1:44)
9. A (I Sam. 6:13, 14)
10. H (I Sam. 31:8-12)

6. Bethel

1. F (II Kings 2:22, 23)
2. D (I Kings 12:25–29)
3. I (Gen. 12:8)
4. H (Josh. 8:12)
5. J (Gen. 35:8)
6. B (I Sam. 30:26, 27)
7. E (Gen. 28:11–19)
8. C (Amos 7:11–13)
9. G (I Sam. 7:16)
10. A (II Kings 23:15, 16)

7. Bible Places

1. Cana (John 2:1–11)
2. Achor (Josh. 7:24–26)
3. Ramah (I Sam. 25:1)
4. Hebron (Josh. 14:14)
5. Nod (Gen. 4:16)
6. Damascus (Acts 9:22–25)
7. Sodom (Gen. 19:24, 25)
8. Mamre (Gen. 18:1)
9. Egypt (Gen. 37:28)
10. Tyre (I Kings 5:1)

8. Bible Rivers

1. E (Josh. 3)
2. A (Num. 22:36)
3. G (Jer. 13:4)
4. B (Ezek. 3:15)
5. J (Gen. 2:10, 11)
6. C (II Kings 5:11, 12)
7. D (Dan. 10:4)
8. F (Gen. 32:22)
9. H (Judg. 4:13)
10. I (Exod. 2:3)

9. Bird, Beast, and Bug Places

1. Cherith brook (I Kings 17:5, 6)
2. Wilderness of Sin (Exod. 16:1, 13)
3. Mount Ararat (Gen. 8:4, 8)
4. Bethel (II Kings 2:23, 24)
5. Timnah (Judg. 14:5)
6. Egypt (I Kings 10:28)
7. Edom (Isa. 34:5, 10, 11)
8. Judean wilderness (Matt. 3:1, 4)
9. Shechem (I Kings 12:1, 14)
10. Egypt (Exod. 8:16–24)

10. Birthplaces

1. C (Gen. 11:27, 28)
2. E (Acts 22:3)
3. G (Acts 4:36)
4. F (I Kings 19:16)
5. I (Gen. 35:26)
6. H (Matt. 2:1)
7. B (Acts 18:24)
8. J (I Chron. 3:1, 2)
9. D (Gen. 46:20)
10. A (Acts 18:2)

11. Brooks

1. Kidron (II Sam. 15:14, 23)
2. 200 (I Sam. 30:9, 10)
3. Elijah (I Kings 17:3)
4. grapes (Num. 13:24)
5. 38 (Deut. 2:13, 14)
6. David (I Sam. 17:19, 40, 49, 50)
7. Elijah (I Kings 18:40)
8. Nehemiah (Neh. 2:11–15)
9. Cedron (John 18:1)
10. Ahab & Obadiah (I Kings 18:5)

12. Burial Places

1. Samuel (I Sam. 25:1)
2. Asa (II Chron. 16:11–14)
3. Joshua (Judg. 2:8, 9)
4. Rachel (Gen. 35:19)
5. Abner (II Sam. 3:30, 32)
6. Jabesh (I Sam. 31:12, 13)
7. Shechem (Josh. 24:32)
8. Manasseh & Amon (II Kings 21:18, 26)
9. Miriam (Num. 20:1)
10. Deborah (Gen. 35:8)
11. Bethany (John 11:1, 44)
12. Sarah (Gen. 23:19)

13. Cast-Aways

1. C (Gen. 21:15)
2. E (Dan. 6:16)
3. G (Jer. 38:6)
4. F (Job 30:19)
5. I (Dan. 3:20, 21)
6. H (Matt. 4:12)
7. B (Matt. 22:11, 13)
8. J (Josh. 10:23, 27)
9. D (Jonah 1:15)
10. A (Gen. 37:24)

14. Castles and Palaces

1. F (I Kings 16:17, 18)
2. I (II Chron. 27:1, 4)
3. J (Isa. 34:5, 13)
4. A (Acts 23:9–11)
5. H (Dan. 5:5, 7)
6. G (Esther 1:5, 6)
7. E (I Kings 22:38, 39)
8. B (I Chron. 11:5, 7)
9. D (Ezra 6:2, 3)
10. C (Jer. 49:27)

15. Caves

1. Makkedah (Josh. 10:16)
2. Machpelah (Gen. 23:9)
3. Mt. Horeb (I Kings 19:8, 9)
4. Lot (Gen. 19:30)
5. Engedi (I Sam. 24)
6. Samaria (I Kings 18:2, 4)
7. Midian (Judg. 6:2)
8. Adullum (I Sam. 22:1, 2)
9. Bethany (John 11:18, 38, 41–44)

16. Cities in Trouble

1. Ai (Josh. 8:18, 19)
2. Ephesus (Acts 19:24–29)
3. Shechem (Judg. 9:34, 45)
4. Philippi (Acts 16:12, 26)
5. Samaria (II Kings 6:24, 25)
6. Jerusalem (II Chron. 32:2–4)
7. Ashdod (I Sam. 5:6)
8. Penuel (Judg. 8:17)
9. Sodom & Gomorrah (Gen. 19:24, 25)
10. Jericho (Josh. 6:1–20)

17. City Acrostic

1. Corinth (Acts 18:1–3)
2. Antioch (Acts 11:26)
3. Paphos (Acts 13:6–11)
4. Ephesus (Acts 19:24, 25)
5. Rome (Acts 28:16, 30)
6. Nineveh (Jonah 1:2)
7. Ai (Josh. 8:1–25)
8. Uz (Job 1:1)
9. Marah (Exod. 15:22–25)

18. City Signposts

1. C (Deut. 34:3)
2. H (Isa. 23:8)
3. J (Isa. 60:14)
4. G (II Sam. 12:27)
5. F (Jonah 3:2)
6. I (Isa. 14:4)
7. E (I Sam. 22:19)
8. A (Zech. 8:3)
9. B (II Chron. 8:4)
10. D (I Chron. 6:57)

21. Egypt

1. Moses (Exod. 2:10; Acts 7:22)
2. Abram (Gen. 12:10)
3. Ezekiel (Ezek. 29:8–12)
4. Joseph (Matt. 2:13)
5. Joseph (Gen. 37:28; 41:41–45)
6. Simeon (Gen. 42:24, 33)
7. Jeroboam (I Kings 11:40)
8. Nebuchadnezzar (Jer. 46:2)
9. Jacob (Gen. 46:26)
10. Jeremiah (Jer. 43:8, 9)

19. Damascus

1. Abram (Gen. 15:2)
2. David (II Sam. 8:6)
3. Elijah (I Kings 19:15)
4. Ahab (I Kings 20:34)
5. Naaman (II Kings 5:11, 12)
6. forty (II Kings 8:7–9)
7. Ahaz (II Kings 16:10)
8. Isaiah (Isa. 17:1)
9. Straight (Acts 9:10, 11)
10. Paul (Acts 9:22–25)

22. Events and Places

1. J (Acts 2:41)
2. G (Acts 20:7–12)
3. H (II Kings 9:30–33)
4. C (Luke 9:10–16)
5. I (Acts 28:1–5)
6. A (Dan. 3:16–30)
7. E (I Sam. 17:4, 42–51)
8. B (II Kings 6:8–20)
9. D (Judg. 7:1–6)
10. F (Josh. 6:1, 20)

20. David's Places of Refuge

1. Ramah (I Sam. 19:10, 18)
2. Gath (I Sam. 21:10)
3. Adullam (I Sam. 22:1)
4. Nob (I Sam. 21:1, 2)
5. Ziph (I Sam. 23:15)
6. Paran (I Sam. 25:1)
7. Maon (I Sam. 23:25)
8. Hareth (I Sam. 22:5)
9. Engedi (I Sam. 23:29)
10. Naioth (I Sam. 19:18)

23. Fields

1. Machpelah (Gen. 23:13–20)
2. Zophim (Num. 23:13, 14)
3. Bethlehem (Ruth 1:22; 2:2, 3)
4. Bethshemesh (I Sam. 6:10–14)
5. Bethlehem (Luke 2:4, 8–11)
6. Anathoth (Jer. 32:7–9)
7. Edom (Num. 20:14–18)
8. Jerusalem (Isa. 36:2)
9. Aceldama (Acts 1:18, 19)
10. Gilgal (II Kings 4:38, 39)

24. Forests and Woods

1. Jotham (II Chron. 27:1, 4)
2. Absalom (II Sam. 18:17)
3. Jonathan (I Sam. 14:24–27)
4. David (I Sam. 22:4, 5)
5. Solomon (I Kings 7:1, 2)
6. Asaph (Neh. 2:8)
7. Ezekiel (Ezek. 20:47)
8. Asa (I Kings 15:11, 13)
9. Abram (Gen. 13:18)
10. two tribes of Joseph (Josh. 17:14–18)

25. Found in the Mountains

1. partridge (I Sam. 26:20)
2. brass (Deut. 8:9)
3. beacon (Isa. 30:17)
4. roes (I Chron. 12:8)
5. vines (Jer. 31:5)
6. stone (Dan. 2:45)
7. herbs (Prov. 27:25)
8. horses & chariots (II Kings 6:17)
9. wine (Amos 9:13)
10. sheep (Ezek. 34:6)
11. banner (Isa. 13:2)
12. corn (Ps. 72:16)

26. Garden of Eden

1. east (Gen. 2:8)
2. river with four branches ran through the garden (Gen. 2:10)
3. Pishon, Gihon, Tigris, Euphrates (Gen. 2:10–14)
4. tree of the knowledge of good and evil (Gen. 2:16, 17)
5. in its midst (Gen. 3:3)
6. "To dress it and to keep it" (Gen. 2:15)
7. Cherubim and flaming sword (Gen. 3:24)
8. "to keep the way of the tree of life" (Gen. 3:24)
9. garden of God (Ezek. 28:13)
10. garden of the Lord (Isa. 51:3)

27. Garden Spots

1. Eden (Gen. 2:8)
2. Jezreel (I Kings 21:1, 2)
3. Jerusalem (II Kings 21:1, 18)
4. Lot (Gen. 13:10, 11)
5. Shushan (Esther 1:5)
6. Jeremiah (Jer. 29:1, 5)
7. Isaiah (Isa. 1:8)
8. Peter (John 18:26)
9. Egypt (Deut. 11:10)
10. Joseph of Arimathaea (John 19:38–42)

28. Gates

1. G (Jer. 39:4)
2. E (Neh. 8:1–3)
3. J (Gen. 19:1)
4. I (II Sam. 15:2–6)
5. A (II Sam. 18:4)
6. C (Gen. 23:16–18)
7. F (Jer. 20:1, 2)
8. D (Ruth 4:1–9)
9. H (Judg. 16:3)
10. B (Exod. 32:26)

29. Geographical Math

1. C (Exod. 28:15, 20)
2. H (Jer. 22:14)
3. J (Isa. 5:10)
4. G (Rev. 3:7)
5. F (I Kings 6:1, 3)
6. I (Deut. 8:15)
7. E (I Tim. 3:1–7)
8. A (II Sam. 5:11)
9. B (Ezek. 45:10, 11)
10. D (Deut. 11:30)

30. God of the Hills

1. melted (Ps. 97:5)
2. quake (Nah. 1:5)
3. singing (Isa. 55:12)
4. setteth (Ps. 65:6)
5. overturneth (Job 28:9)
6. smoke (Ps. 104:32)
7. depart & removed (Isa. 54:10)
8. trembled (Hab. 3:10)
9. flowed (Isa. 64:3)
10. molten (Mic. 1:4)

33. Hidden Mountains

1. Ebal
2. Sinai
3. Hermon
4. Seir
5. Nebo
6. Bethel
7. Hor
8. Tabor
9. Gilead
10. Ararat

31. God's Commands

1. Jonah (Jonah 1:2)
2. Moses (Deut. 1:3; 3:27)
3. David (I Sam. 23:4)
4. Elijah (I Kings 17:9)
5. Jacob (Gen. 35:1)
6. Ananias (Acts 9:10, 11)
7. Jeremiah (Jer. 13:6)
8. Saul (Paul) (Acts 22:10)
9. Abraham (Gen. 22:2)
10. Joshua (Josh. 8:1)

34. High Places

1. C (Gen. 8:4)
2. E (II Chron. 3:1)
3. G (Judges 2:8,9)
4. F (I Sam. 31:8)
5. I (II Sam. 15:30)
6. H (Num. 20:25, 26)
7. B (II Kings 4:25)
8. J (Num. 23:11–14)
9. D (Exod. 19:18–21)
10. A (I Kings 19:8, 11)

32. Hidden Cities and Towns

1. Tarsus
2. Tyre
3. Gath
4. Nain
5. Bethel
6. Sodom
7. Ramah
8. Damascus
9. Rome
10. Athens

35. Hills in Prophecy

1. low (Isa. 40:4)
2. moved lightly (Jer. 4:24)
3. removed (Isa. 54:10)
4. crashing (Zeph. 1:10)
5. melt (Amos 9:13)
6. break (Isa. 55:12)
7. bow (Hab. 3:6)
8. fall (Hos. 10:8)
9. flow (Joel 3:18)
10. lifted up (Isa. 2:12, 14)

36. Hometowns

1. J (Acts 9:36)
2. G (Amos 1:1)
3. H (Josh. 2:1–15)
4. C (Jer. 1:1)
5. I (John 11:1)
6. A (Acts 10:1)
7. E (Luke 2:33, 39)
8. B (II Kings 22:14)
9. D (I Sam. 7:17)
10. F (John 1:44)

37. Who Said It?

1. J (Dan. 4:28, 30)
2. G (Jer. 8:22)
3. H (II Chron. 2:16)
4. C (Josh. 15:16)
5. I (Ezra 8:15)
6. A (II Sam. 23:15)
7. E (Gen. 47:29)
8. B (Gal. 1:18)
9. D (John 1:46)
10. F (II Kings 5:12)

38. Wilderness Places

1. Gibeon (II Sam. 2:24)
2. Jeruel (II Chron. 20:14–26)
3. Shur (Exod. 15:22)
4. Beersheba (Gen. 21:14)
5. Paran (Gen. 21:21)
6. Sinai (Num. 3:4)
7. Maon (I Sam. 23:25)
8. Judea (Matt. 3:1)
9. Damascus (I Kings 19:15)
10. Kadesh (Ps. 29:8)

39. How Long?

1. 7 days (Ezek. 3:15)
2. 20 years (I Sam. 7:1, 2)
3. 3 days (Acts 9:8, 9)
4. 430 years (Exod. 12:40)
5. 40 days (Num. 13:25)
6. 7 days (Josh. 6:15)
7. 52 days (Neh. 6:15)
8. 3 years (II Sam. 13:38)
9. 1 hour (Rev. 18:19)

40. In the Valleys

1. Salt (II Sam. 8:13)
2. Sorek (Judg. 16:4)
3. Hebron (Gen. 37:14)
4. Lebanon (Josh. 11:17)
5. Baca (Ps. 84:6)
6. Elah (I Sam. 17:2)
7. Eshcol (Num. 32:9)
8. Keziz (Josh. 18:21)
9. Achor (Isa. 65:10)
10. Shaveh (Gen. 14:17)

41. Israelite's Wilderness Wandering

1. C (Exod. 15:22–25)
2. G (Exod. 15:27)
3. E (Exod. 16:2–18)
4. B (Num. 11:33, 34)
5. J (Num. 11:35; 12:10–16)
6. H (Num. 13:2, 3)
7. I (Exod. 17:1–7)
8. D (Exod. 17:8–13)
9. A (Exod. 19:20; 20:1–26)
10. F (Deut. 34:1, 5, 6)

42. Jericho

1. C (II Kings 2:18–22)
2. E (Josh. 5:13–15)
3. G (Mark 10:46–52)
4. F (II Kings 25:4–7)
5. I (I Kings 16:34)
6. H (Josh. 6:17–25)
7. B (II Kings 2:4, 11)
8. J (Judg. 3:12–22)
9. D (Luke 19:1–7)
10. A (II Sam. 10:4, 5)

43. Jerusalem: The Golden

1. Benjamin (Josh. 18:28)
2. Jebus (Judg. 19:10)
3. David (II Sam. 5:6–9)
4. Solomon (I Kings 5–7)
5. Shishak (I Kings 14:25, 26)
6. Uzziah (II Chron. 26:9)
7. Hezekiah (II Kings 20:20)
8. Nebuchadnezzar (II Kings 25)
9. Nehemiah
10. Jeremiah (19–20:1, 2)

44. Jerusalem's Gates

1. first (Zech. 14:10)
2. king (I Chron. 9:18)
3. east (Neh. 3:29)
4. sheep (Neh. 3:32)
5. water (Neh. 3:26)
6. dung (Neh. 3:14)
7. corner (Zech. 14:10)
8. horse (Neh. 3:28)
9. fish (Neh. 3:3)
10. old (Neh. 3:6)

45. Jesus' Miracles Geographically

1. C (John 2:1–11)
2. A (John 11:1–44)
3. D (Luke 4:31, 38, 39)
4. I (Luke 7:11–15)
5. H (Luke 5:1–9)
6. F (Mark 5:1–13)
7. E (Mark 7:31–37)
8. B (Mark 8:22–26)
9. J (Luke 17:11–19)
10. G (John 5:1–9)

46. "K" Places

1. J (Num. 20:1)
2. G (Num. 11:31–35)
3. H (I Kings 15:11–13)
4. C (Judg. 8:10, 11)
5. I (I Sam. 7:2)
6. A (Judg. 4:9, 10)
7. E (II Sam. 23:20)
8. B (I Kings 18:40)
9. D (I Sam. 23:1–5)
10. F (Josh. 15:16, 17)

47. Land 'Em in Their Land

1. C (Gen. 22:2)
2. E (Matt. 14:25, 34)
3. D (I Sam. 9:5)
4. F (I Kings 9:11)
5. A (Gen. 4:16)
6. J (II Kings 19:36, 37)
7. B (Job 1:1)
8. I (Deut. 34:5)
9. H (Num. 13:2, 6)
10. G (Gen. 47:1–6)

48. Land of Canaan

1. Immanuel
2. Hebrews
3. Lord's
4. promise
5. Israel
6. Palestina
7. holy
8. glorious
9. Jews
10. Beulah

49. Little Town of Bethlehem

1. Joseph & Mary (Luke 2:4, 5)
2. Naomi & Ruth (Ruth 1:22)
3. Samuel (I Sam. 16:1–4)
4. Micah (Mic. 5:2)
5. Rehoboam (II Chron. 11:5, 6, 11)
6. Asahel (II Sam. 2:23, 32)
7. killed every baby, two years and under (Matt. 2:16)
8. Boaz (Ruth 1:22; 2:1)
9. Rachel (Gen. 35:19, 20)
10. David (I Chron. 11:17)

50. New Jerusalem

1. "Coming down from God out of heaven" (Rev. 21:2)
2. pure gold (Rev. 21:18)
3. "Wall great and high" (Rev. 21:12)
4. jasper (Rev. 21:18)
5. twelve (Rev. 21:14)
6. "all manner of precious stones" (Rev. 21:19)
7. 12 apostles (Rev. 21:14)
8. twelve (Rev. 21:12)
9. pearl (Rev. 21:21)
10. pure transparent gold (Rev. 21:21)
11. temple (Rev. 21:22)
12. sun or moon to light it (Rev. 21:23)

51. Nineveh

1. Asshur (Gen. 10:11)
2. Sennacherib (II Kings 19:36)
3. Jonah (Jonah 1:2)
4. forty (Jonah 3:4)
5. He passed a decree that everyone was to put on sackcloth and fast. (Jonah 3:6–8)
6. sixscore thousand (120,000) (Jonah 4:11)
7. Nahum (Nah. 1–3)
8. flood & fire (Nah. 1:8; 3:13, 15)
9. Zephaniah (Zeph. 2:13)
10. Jesus (Matt. 12:41)

52. Pa and Ma Places

1. Patmos (Rev. 1:9)
2. Maon (I Sam. 25:2, 3)
3. Paran (Num. 13:1–3)
4. Mamre (Gen. 18:1, 2)
5. Paphos (Acts 13:6)
6. Marah (Exod. 15:23–25)
7. Padan-aram (Gen. 28:1, 2)
8. Machpelah (Gen. 23:4–9)
9. Pamphylia (Acts 13:13)
10. Macedonia (Acts 16:9)

53. Pillars

1. Samuel (I Sam. 7:12)
2. Moses (Exod. 24:4)
3. Rachel (Gen. 35:19, 20)
4. Absalom (II Sam. 18:18)
5. Jachin & Boaz (I Kings 7:21)
6. Abimelech (Judg. 9:6)
7. Jacob (Gen. 28:18, 22)
8. Adonijah (I Kings 1:9)
9. Isaiah (Isa. 19:19)
10. Laban & Jacob (Gen. 31:44–53)

54. Place Names in Threes

1. Nod (Gen. 4:16)
2. Zin (Num. 13:21)
3. Hor (Num. 20:27, 28)
4. Nob (I Sam. 22:18, 19)
5. Luz (Gen. 35:6, 7)
6. Dan (I Kings 12:26–29)
7. Kir (II Kings 16:9)
8. Ono (Neh. 6:2)
9. Sin (Exod. 16:1–4)
10. Tob (Judg. 11:3)

55. Places of Disaster

1. Siloam (Luke 13:4)
2. Gaza (Judg. 16:21–30)
3. Ai (Josh. 8:24, 25)
4. Ophrah (Judg. 9:5)
5. Kishon brook (I Kings 18:19, 40)
6. Aphek (I Kings 20:30)
7. Bethlehem (Matt. 2:16)
8. Red Sea (Exod. 14:26–28)
9. wilderness (Num. 16:41–49)
10. Mizpah (Jer. 41:5–8)

56. Places of Kings

1. David (I Sam. 22:1)
2. Jeroboam (I Kings 12:25–29)
3. Uzziah (II Chron. 26:10)
4. Ahaz (II Kings 16:10–12)
5. Pharoah (Gen. 47:22–26)
6. Ishbosheth (II Sam. 2:8, 9)
7. Solomon (II Chron. 8:3, 4)
8. Nebuchadnezzar (II Kings 24:11)
9. Asa (I Kings 15:13)
10. Amaziah (II Kings 14:18, 19)
11. Josiah (II Kings 23:29)
12. Sennacherib (II Kings 19:36, 37)

57. Plains

1. Nehemiah (Neh. 6:2)
2. Nebuchadnezzar (Dan. 3:1)
3. Abram (Gen. 13:18)
4. Saul (I Sam. 10:3)
5. Joshua (Josh. 4:13, 14)
6. Moses (Deut. 34:1)
7. David (II Sam. 15:27, 28, 30)
8. Lot (Gen. 13:10, 11)
9. Heber (Judg. 4:11)
10. Jordan (I Kings 7:45, 46)

58. Pools

1. F (John 9:6, 7)
2. I (Neh. 2:13, 14)
3. J (II Sam. 4:5–12)
4. A (I Kings 22:37, 38)
5. H (II Kings 18:17, 18)
6. G (Song of Sol. 7:4)
7. E (II Sam. 2:12–16)
8. B (John 5:2–4)
9. D (Isa. 22:9)
10. C (Exod. 7:19)

59. Prophet Places

1. Elisha (II Kings 2:19–22)
2. Ezekiel (Ezek. 1:1)
3. Jonah (Jonah 1:1, 2)
4. Jeremiah (Jer. 13:4, 5)
5. Daniel (Dan. 6:10)
6. Elijah (I Kings 17:3, 4)
7. Amos (Amos 1:1)
8. Isaiah (Isa. 19:23)
9. Micah (Mic. 1:6)
10. Obadiah (Obad. 1:1)

60. River Jordan

1. Naaman (II Kings 5:10–14)
2. Jesus (Matt. 3:13–16)
3. Elisha (II Kings 6:1–7)
4. Gideon (Judg. 8:4)
5. Joshua (Josh. 4:8, 9)
6. Elijah (II Kings, 2:7, 8)
7. three (Josh. 3:16, 17; 4:18; II Kings 2:6–8, 13, 14)
8. David (II Sam. 19:16–18)
9. Ehud (Judg. 3:26–29)
10. Moses (Deut. 31:1, 2)

61. Rivers of the Bible

1. Kishon (Judg. 5:21)
2. Ulai (Dan. 8:16)
3. Gihon (Gen. 2:13)
4. Arnon (Josh. 12:1)
5. Pharpar (II Kings 5:12)
6. Chebar (Ezek. 1:1)
7. Kanah (Josh. 16:8)
8. Ahava (Ezra 8:21)
9. Pishon (Gen. 2:11)
10. Abana (II Kings 5:12)

62. Sacred Places

1. Mt. Horeb (Exod. 3:1, 5)
2. Bethel (Gen. 35:14, 15)
3. Mt. Moriah (II Chron. 3:1)
4. Ophrah (Judg. 6:11–24)
5. Mt. Gerizim (Deut. 11:29)
6. Shiloh (Josh. 18:1)
7. Jerusalem (II Chron. 26:14–19)
8. Jericho (Josh. 5:13–15)
9. city of David (I Chron. 15:1)
10. Mt. Carmel (I Kings 18:9–39)

63. Samaria

1. Omri (I Kings 16:23, 24)
2. Ahab (I Kings 16:29–32)
3. king of Israel & Jehoshaphat (I Kings 22:10)
4. Ahaziah (II Kings 1:2)
5. Elisha (II Kings 6:14–20)
6. Ben-hadad (II Kings 6:24, 25)
7. four (II Kings 7:1, 3)
8. Micah (Mic. 1:6)
9. Philip, Peter, John (Acts 8:5–25)
10. Simon (Acts 8:9)

64. Scrambled Countries

1. J Egypt (Gen. 42:1, 2)
2. G Syria (II Kings 5:1)
3. H Mesopotamia (I Chron. 19:6, 7)
4. C Ophir (I Kings 9:28)
5. I Italy (Acts 18:2)
6. D Armenia (II Kings 19:36, 37)
7. B Arabia (II Chron. 9:14)
8. F Ethiopia (Jer. 38:7–13)
9. A Macedonia (Acts 16:9)
10. E Moab (I Sam. 22:3, 4)

65. Scrambled Islands

1. Patmos (Rev. 1:9)
2. Cyprus (Acts 13:4)
3. Clauda (Acts 27:16)
4. Rhodes (Acts 21:1)
5. Chios (Acts 20:15)
6. Crete (Acts 27:7)
7. Melita (Acts 28:1)
8. Samos (Acts 20:15)
9. Cos (Acts 21:1)
10. Samothracia (Acts 16:11)

66. Seas

1. third day (Gen. 1:9, 10)
2. Salt (Gen. 14:3)
3. Moses (Exod. 15:1, 4)
4. cedar (Ezra 3:7)
5. Jeremiah (Jer. 48:32)
6. Sea of Galilee (John 6:1, 16–19)
7. Tiberias (John 21:1)
8. Adria (Acts 27:27)
9. John (Rev. 4:6)
10. Mediterranean

67. Streets

1. Ahab & Ben-hadad (I Kings 20:34)
2. Saul & Jonathan (II Sam. 21:12)
3. Jeremiah (Jer. 37:21)
4. John (Rev. 21:21)
5. Ananias (Acts 9:10, 11)
6. Hezekiah (II Chron. 29:1, 4)
7. Zechariah (Zech. 8:5)
8. Lot (Gen. 19:1, 2)
9. David (II Sam. 1:17, 20)
10. Peter (Acts 12:8–10)
11. Ezra (Neh. 8:1–3)
12. Job (Job 29:7, 8)

68. The Name Was Changed

1. E (Gen. 28:19)
2. H (Judg. 18:29)
3. B (Gen. 23:2)
4. I (Gen. 14:8)
5. J (Gen. 35:19)
6. A (Josh. 15:15)
7. D (II Sam. 5:7)
8. F (Judg. 1:17)
9. C (I Chron. 11:4)
10. G (II Chron. 20:2)

69. Towers

1. Edar (Gen. 35:21)
2. Syene (Ezek. 29:10)
3. Penuel (Judg. 8:17)
4. Hananeel (Jer. 31:38)
5. David (Song of Sol. 4:4)
6. Siloam (Luke 13:4)
7. Jezreel (II Kings 9:17)
8. Shechem (Judg. 9:49)
9. Meah (Neh. 12:39)
10. Lebanon (Song of Sol. 7:4)

70. Unusual Sights

1. G (Josh. 10:12–14)
2. D (Acts 9:3–9)
3. H (II Kings 6:1–7)
4. J (Exod. 3:1, 2)
5. I (Exod. 7:2, 3, 10)
6. C (Judg. 14:5–8)
7. A (II Kings 6:13–17)
8. B (Exod. 17:6)
9. F (Dan. 5:5, 7)
10. E (Acts 10:8, 11, 12)

71. Watering Places

1. Harod (Judg. 7:1–6)
2. Cherith (I Kings 17:3, 4)
3. Elim (Exod. 15:27)
4. plain of Jordan (Gen. 13:9–11)
5. Jerusalem (II Kings 18:2; 20:20)
6. Jericho (II Kings 2:18–22)
7. Bahurim (II Sam. 17:17–19)
8. Bethesda (John 5:2, 4)
9. valley of Gerar (Gen. 26:17, 19)
10. Mesopotamia (Gen. 24:10–18)

72. What Was Where?

1. F (Num. 21:4, 9)
2. D (Gen. 28:12, 19)
3. I (Exod. 24:4)
4. H (Gen. 2:9, 17)
5. J (Acts 19)
6. B (Josh. 4:5–9)
7. E (Deut. 3:11)
8. C (Dan. 3:1)
9. G (II Kings 12:1, 9)
10. A (Num. 23:14)

73. Where?

1. G (Acts 9:10, 11)
2. D (Josh. 2:1, 15)
3. H (Ezek. 28:13)
4. J (I Kings 22:38, 39)
5. I (Gen. 11:2, 4)
6. C (Acts 28:16, 30)
7. A (Dan. 3:1, 20)
8. B (Acts 1:19)
9. F (Acts 10:5, 6)
10. E (Mark 2:1, 14)

74. Why?

1. Because he had wholly followed God (Josh. 14:14)
2. King Artaxerxes, complying with wishes of opponents of the Jews, issued an order to stop the work (Ezra 4:7–24).
3. They saw Peter heal a palsied man (Acts 9:32–35).
4. "There was much water there" (John 3:23).
5. He did not ask their help to fight the Ammonites (Judg. 12:1).
6. To salute Festus (Acts 25:13)
7. To save him from his enemies (Acts 9:29, 30)
8. So that Isaiah's prophecy might be fulfilled (Matt. 4:13–15)
9. Because a famine had destroyed their pasture land in Canaan (Gen. 47:1–4)
10. It was the site his father David had selected for a temple (II Chron. 3:1).
11. "That it might be fulfilled which was spoken by the prophets 'He shall be called a Nazarene'" (Matt. 2:19–23)
12. Because Paul had cured a demoniac slave girl (Acts 16:16–24)